DIY Vegan Protein Bars:

25 Vegan Protein Bar Recipes to Build Muscle, Burn Fat and Stay healthy

By

ProjectVegan

Table of Contents

Introduction 3

Chapter 1: What is Veganism? 4

Chapter 2: The Importance of Protein in Your Diet 7

Chapter 3: Sources of Proteins Vegans Need to Know About 9

Chapter 4: Veganism and Bodybuilding 13

Chapter 5: 20 Tips for the Vegan Bodybuilder! 15

Chapter 6: Vegan Protein Bar Recipes 19

Conclusion: 40

Introduction

This book will guide you through the concept of veganism, the significance of protein in a vegan diet and how, by concentrating on high protein foods and following simple tips, one can actually become a successful bodybuilder. Also, if you are not a vegan but are thinking of becoming one, you will be totally convinced of the benefits of veganism. One of the most well-known personalities in vegan bodybuilding, Robert Cheeke, has been at the frontline of ushering in an unusual way to stimulate and nurture bodybuilders in a society thriving on animal products for body mass enhancement. Protein bars and shakes are a great add-on to your diet to make certain you're getting ample amounts of protein. You will find in this book very easy to follow homemade protein bar recipes that you will definitely want to try at home. These protein bars are not only high in energy and fiber, but are also delicious and low in calories.

Here Is a Preview of what you'll find…
- What is veganism?
- The difference between a vegan diet and veganism
- The importance of protein in our diet
- Rich sources of protein for vegans
- Tips to build muscles on a vegan diet
- Recipes for vegan protein bars

Chapter 1: What is Veganism?

Veganism can be described as a way of life in which its followers practice the exclusion of animals and their by-products, be it for food, clothing, entertainment or for any other purpose. The concept of veganism has spread widely throughout the population due to various reasons, mainly for health benefits, environmental or ethical factors. Awareness of veganism has increased as many popular books and movies encourage this way of living. Also, the availability of vegan foods in restaurants and supermarkets in many countries is increasing, making veganism a viable diet to follow.

The word vegan was invented by Donald Watson (in 1944), the co-founder of the Vegan Society in England, to mean "non-dairy vegetarian" and later on to submit to "the principle that man should survive without abusing animals." Vegans rely entirely on food obtained from plant sources, as they oppose the exploitation of and cruelty to animals, hence do not include flesh, fish, eggs, milk and other animal by-products in their diet. Instead they encourage the use of alternatives for the same benefits. Some vegans in addition to avoiding all animal derived products, detest animals being kept in captivity, training and using animals for entertainment purposes as in zoos, circuses, races or in rodeos.

The different categories of vegans include ovo-lacto vegans, dietary vegans, ethical and environmental vegans. Dietary vegans, unlike ovo-lacto vegans, abstain from not only consuming animals and dairy products but also from substances that use any form of animal derivative. Ethical vegans broaden their values beyond food and also refrain from animal exploitation in other aspects of their daily life, such as in clothes, medicine and cosmetics. Ethical vegans also avoid beeswax, wool, silk, shellac, fur, leather, and many other animal-based products, as they are of the view that animal use for amusement or eating is uncalled for and brutal.

Environmental vegans believe that harvesting or industrial farming, the existing technique for meat, dairy and egg production, causes irreparable environmental damage, and a plant-based diet is a more ecologically friendly choice for the future of the Earth.

What's the difference between veganism and a vegan diet?

While veganism is a way of life that aims to exclude reliance on or the misuse of animals as much as possible while still existing in the modern world, many people have taken up a vegan diet without consideration or awareness of ethical veganism. Therefore, a person who only follows a vegan diet for one of the above reasons and not veganism may still buy and wear silk, woolen or leather clothes or use articles made out of animal skin like belts, bags, purses, etc. or take pleasure in going to circuses, rodeos or aquariums. They may also use inedible products tested on animals or keep animals as pets. A vegan diet is just a way of eating; a diet that is devoid of all animal and derived by-products. The reason for people to pursue a vegan diet may be either on the basis of personal preference, ethical or religious background, for health benefits or maybe to avoid allergies.

 A vegan diet hence includes foods like fruits, vegetables, nuts, whole grains, seeds and products extracted from plants like oils, beverages, sugars, etc., but exclude all animal products, such as beef, dairy, fish, eggs, poultry, honey and gelatin; although some dietary vegans do consume honey.

 A well designed vegan diet has many health benefits and decreases the risk of chronic heart diseases and is regarded as an apt diet for all phases of one's life. Vegan diets are likely to be high in folic acid vitamin E, iron, vitamin C, dietary fibers, magnesium, and phytochemicals, while low in saturated fat, cholesterol, omega-3 fatty acids, zinc, calcium, vitamin D and vitamin B12. Many leading dietitians and food experts advocate eating vitamin B12 fortified foods, such as soy milk and fortified cereals, or take supplements to get ample quantities of this vitamin, which is chiefly found in animal products.

The rising recognition of veganism has made it easier than ever to go vegan, with innumerable resources and vegan substitute foods now accessible.

Chapter 2: The Importance of Protein in Your Diet

Protein is a macronutrient and a very important constituent of a balanced diet as:
- It is a constituent of all body cells. As a matter of fact, nails and hair are typically made of protein.
- It is required to repair and build tissue.
- Hormones, enzymes, and many other important body chemicals are made up of protein.
- It is a vital building block of cartilage, muscles, bones, skin, and blood.
- It is required in comparatively large quantities to maintain health.
- Our bodies do not stock up on protein like they do carbohydrates and fats, hence it has no reserve to draw from when the dietary requirement is not being met.

Benefits of a Protein-Enriched Diet
Consuming high-protein foods has many benefits, including:
- Speedy revitalization after work outs
- Reducing muscle loss
- Building muscle mass
- Helping you maintain a healthy weight
- Reducing appetite

As we all know that rich sources of protein usually include animal products, and also that vegans acquire all their proteins from plant sources, a common question that arises is whether vegans are able to meet their daily requirements of proteins and also whether plant protein provides sufficient quantities of the essential amino acids that cannot be manufactured in the human body.

Sources of plant protein include legumes such as peas, black beans, soy beans – popular forms include edamame, tempeh, soy milk and tofu, and chickpeas - often eaten as hummus; grains such as corn, bulgur quinoa, brown rice, barley, and wheat-often eaten as seitan and whole-wheat bread; and seeds and nuts, such as sunflower seeds hemp, flax and almonds, peanuts etc.

Quinoa and soy beans are complete proteins since they both have all the important amino acids in quantities that meet human demands.

Protein in Muscle Growth and Maintenance –

If you want to build up and retain muscle mass, you must consume sufficient amounts of nutritional protein. But did you know that eating protein throughout the day might be the most effective way to build muscle? Whether you're a bodybuilder wanting to build muscle mass or just concerned about maintaining muscle with age, it may be useful to aim for about 30 grams of protein per meal, three times a day.

Protein and Bone Health –

Proteins taken in the diet play a key role in both bone and muscle repair. Tough muscles help guard against bone diseases, and consumption of adequate protein guards against muscle wasting with age. Dietary protein stimulates the production of growth hormones that fortify bone and muscle, as well as boosts calcium assimilation. In elderly people, more than the existing Recommended Dietary Allowance (RDA) is recommended, as they require more protein to build and retain muscle than do younger people.

Chapter 3: Sources of Proteins Vegans Need to Know About

There is strong evidence advocating the consumption of meat-free foods not only because they are cheaper and lower in calories, but also good for your health and the environment. But the main concern remains: Is it possible to get enough complete proteins on a totally plant-based diet?

The word "complete protein" refers to amino acids, the building blocks of protein. There are 20 diverse amino acids that can make a protein, and nine that the body can't manufacture on its own. These are called the indispensable amino acids—we require them in our diet since we can't build them ourselves. For it to be considered "complete," a protein should include all nine of these necessary amino acids in approximately identical quantities.

Many animal products like meat and eggs are complete proteins, whereas nuts and beans aren't. But since we need only a small amount of these essential amino acids daily, many dieticians believe that, since plant-based diets include such an extensive range of foods, vegans are nearly assured of getting all of their amino acids easily. Vegan diets are mostly based on vegetables, fruits and nuts, grains and other seeds, legumes (particularly beans), meat substitutes based on wheat-based seitan/gluten or soybeans (tofu).

Rich Sources of Plant Protein Includes:

1. **Quinoa:** contains 8 grams/1 cup serving of protein when cooked.

Quinoa is an excellent alternative for rice, and it's adaptable enough to make muffins, cookies, and breakfast dishes. It is packed with manganese, iron, fiber and magnesium. It is a unique plant-based source of complete protein since it is totally gluten free.

2. **Buckwheat:** contains 6 grams/1 cup serving of protein when cooked.

Buckwheat is eaten either as seeds ground into flour or the hulled kernels similar to oats, or, as in Japan, as noodles. Buckwheat is really nutritious and has been proven to have a positive effect on circulation and in controlling blood glucose and cholesterol levels.

3. **Hempseed:** Contains 10 grams protein/2 tablespoon serving.

This member of the well-known narcotic family contains large quantities of all nine necessary amino acids, as well as iron, calcium, zinc, and magnesium in abundance. They're also a vegan supply of important fatty acids, like omega-3, which can aid in fighting depression without the drug-like effect.

Chia seeds: contain 4 grams protein/2 tablespoon serving.

Chia seeds are an excellent plant source of omega-3 fatty acids, and they have more fiber than nuts or flax seeds. Chia is also a rich source of antioxidants, zinc, iron and calcium. These seeds can be used to make puddings or thicken smoothies, as they form a gel when mixed with water or non dairy milk.

4. **Soy:** contains protein as: 10 grams/½ cup serving (firm tofu), 15 grams/½ cup serving (tempeh), 15 grams/½ cup serving (natto).

Soy is a complete protein. This means they have all the vital amino acids for humans, and can be relied upon entirely for protein intake and is popularly known as the ideal substitute for meat in a vegan diet. Tempeh and natto are made by fermenting soybeans, but tofu is doubtlessly the best known soy product. It is eaten mostly as soy milk and tofu (bean curd), which is soy milk mixed with a coagulant. Tofu comes in a range of consistencies, depending on the water content; hard, solid and semisolid for stir-frying and stews, to soft or silken for desserts, shakes and salad dressings.

5. **Fruits and Vegetables:**

One cup of cooked French beans has about 13 grams of protein; the same serving of spinach has about 7 grams, two cups of cooked kale has about 5 grams. One cup of boiled peas; 9 grams, 1 avocado; 10 grams, 1 cup broccoli; 5 grams.

Rice, lentils and beans (black, kidney, etc): Protein content: 7 grams/1 cup serving.
These are one of the most widely available and low cost vegan meals with large amounts of protein on par with that of meat. Substituting chickpeas or lentils for beans produces the same result. These meals are a great way to bulk up on proteins and carbohydrates after intense exercise.

Seitan: Protein content: 21 grams/1/3 cup serving

Seitan is made by incorporating gluten (the protein in wheat) with water or stock, herbs and spices, and cooking it in a soy-rich broth to add the missing amino acid (lysine) to the tough, meat-like finished product.

Ezekiel Bread: Protein content: 8 grams/2 slice serving

Extraordinarily nutritious bread that contains all of the essential amino acids, usually made from sprouted grains, which considerably boosts the bread's vitamin and fiber content, as well as its digestibility.

6. **Hummus and Pita:** Protein content: 7 grams/1 whole-wheat pita and 2 tbsp. of hummus

A good protein source, especially famous in Mediterranean and Middle Eastern countries; it makes a filling meal. Hummus is usually made from chickpeas but it can also be made from edamame, cannellini, or other kinds of beans.

7. **Spirulina with Grains or Nuts:** Protein content: 4 grams/1 tablespoon

Makes a complete protein meal with plenty of nuts, grains, oats or seeds.
Peanut Butter Sandwich: Protein content: 15 grams/2-slice sandwich with 2 tbsp. of peanut butter

Peanut butter on whole wheat bread is a simple snack that, while quite high in calories, supplies a load of all the necessary amino acids and an abundance of healthy fats. When peanuts and legumes like lentils and beans are consumed with grains like wheat, rice and corn, we obtain a whole protein meal.

Chapter 4: Veganism and Bodybuilding

Whenever you hear of bodybuilders, the impression in your mind is of huge, bulky men (or women) gulping down large portions of chicken breasts, egg whites and milkshakes. But, with time, this concept is changing with many successful vegan body builders and athletes coming to the fore. Vegan world champion athletes include Dave Scott (triathlon) and Carl Lewis (sprinter), Scott Jurek (an ultra-marathoner), and Mike Tyson, world heavyweight ex-boxing champ, who seems to be following a vegan diet these days. Robert Cheeke is one of the most well-known vegan bodybuilders, but there are many others, too. The idea that you need lots of meat to be large, sturdy or powerful is clearly disproved. However, since vegans do not rely on animals or their by-products for their protein requirement, whatever be their reason, it becomes really challenging for vegan bodybuilders to ingest all their dietary nutrients, especially vitamin B12, omega-3 fatty acids, creatine, zinc and iron. However, with some basic strategies and tips, you can quite easily overcome any hurdles.

Strategies for Vegan Bodybuilders and Athletes

As far as diet is concerned, a vegan diet should be properly designed keeping in mind the following:

1. **Protein:** Protein, as we have just read, is extremely important for muscle building, and a daily intake of at least 0.5 grams/pound of body weight is required. Weight lifters, athletes, and bodybuilders require 50% more protein in their diets to compensate for the wear and tear and stress of muscle building. This is because limitations on egg, meat and dairy consumption limit the total protein eaten in comparison to consumption of beans, nuts, grains and vegetables, which provide smaller quantities.

2. Eat plenty of Carbohydrates: Vegans have to make sure they consume sufficient calories to fuel muscle growth and

revival from training. Because plant foods are high in fiber, which can be quite filling, protein and carbohydrate powder supplements may be needed. Vegan diets should typically be high in carbohydrates, in the range of 65-75 percent. A vegan diet should also include above 20% fat by calories so that requirement of 3000-4000 calories a day can be fulfilled, particularly in the post-exercise meal. The consumption of nuts, especially walnuts, almonds and peanuts, may avert possible deficiencies of essential fatty acids.

3. Vitamins and minerals: Vitamin B12, zinc, iron and omega-3. These essential nutrients may be missing in an inadequately planned vegan diet. Calcium is present abundantly in nuts, beans and green leafy vegetables, but vegans must intentionally seek ample sunshine exposure to improve vitamin D assimilation, as it is vital for bone health. Iron and zinc absorption is not as efficient from plant foods as from animal foods, so vegan exercisers and weight trainers need to take multivitamin supplements for solving any possible deficiencies. Also, fortified foods such as soy milk, breakfast cereals and specially devised vegan foods can ensure adequate intake of these vitamins and minerals.

4. **Consider a creatine supplement:** Creatine is a constituent of animal meat and is a bulk and muscle builder. Although it is not a necessary nutrient, it may help build muscle as vegan diets are very low in creatine, hence it must be taken as an add-on by vegans (and also non-vegans).

Chapter 5: 20 Tips for the Vegan Bodybuilder!

Vegan eating: Saying no to meat doesn't imply you have to say no to your fitness or muscle building goals!

If you want to build more muscle mass but prefer eating a vegan diet, you may frequently feel beaten before you even start. In an earlier chapter, we reviewed the types and quantity of food to be included and the missing nutrients that must be supplemented.

Let's now take a look at the top tips that a vegan bodybuilder should find helpful:

1. **Get adequate calories**

A vegan body builder needs to take in ample quantities of calories regularly so that the body does not start utilizing proteins for fuel. This will result in muscle loss.

2. **Eat more often**

A very important tip to be followed is to eat at regular intervals throughout the day. That way you will be assured of receiving a steady supply of amino acids into the muscles.

3. **Avoid too many processed foods**

Eating vegan food does not mean you can freely eat all the processed foods you want; it's important to make an effort to include healthy foods like grains, nuts, fruits, etc. A great way to achieve that is to eat protein bars that are full of energy, too.

4. **Be sure to vary your food choices**

For vegans, it's important to consume a varied diet so that the food is not only appealing but also to prevent any nutritional deficiencies. Regularly eat different types of grains and nuts, or try innovative ways of consuming the same.

Here are some other useful tips:

Eat lots of fruits and vegetables
Fruits and vegetables are loaded with essential vitamins and minerals, and are healthy as they contain antioxidants to help your immune system function properly.

Chickpeas and legumes
Chickpeas (especially in the form of hummus) and legumes are a rich source of proteins and also an excellent source of low-fat carbohydrates that make a good snack prior to an intense workout.

Focus on broccoli and spinach
Take in ample amounts of these two high calcium vegetables, as this is one nutrient you may fall short of as it is commonly found in dairy products. You may also need a supplement to ensure you are receiving enough calcium.

Swap rice for quinoa
Try switching your usual brown rice for quinoa (a combination of oatmeal and brown rice) as it is a source of complete protein and also has high overall protein content that is vital for muscle building.

Make use of tempeh
Another nutritious, highly preferred protein source, tempeh can be a creative way to add protein to your diet.

Utilize nuts for fuel
Nuts are a good supply of fat and a long-lasting form of energy as well. One handful will appreciably perk up your calorie intake and make muscle enhancement easier.

Take in ample amounts of flaxseeds, walnuts, and flaxseed oil
Primary sources for essential fatty acids, since vegans do not consume fatty fish or fish oil, can be flaxseed oil, flaxseed, and walnuts.

Monitor your body fat levels
Regular monitoring of body fat levels will help you give an indication of whether you're losing muscle mass, so steps can be taken to avoid this.

Supplement with branched chain amino acids
Branched chain amino acids are another vital supplement that you may consider using to prevent muscle loss. This should be taken immediately before or after a workout is complete.

Start adding peanut butter
Use peanut butter for boosting overall calorie intake and energy levels, especially when exercising. You can add it to your oatmeal, fruits or any smoothies that you may have.

Consider iron supplementation
Since iron is an important constituent of red blood cells, you may need to take an iron supplement daily because if you have an iron deficiency, workouts may become a lot more tiring and less effective. On a long term vegan diet, this may be a point of concern.

5. Keep your workouts short but concentrated
On a vegan diet, small but intense exercise sessions are usually recommended, mainly to avoid muscle and your body turning to proteins for its energy needs. If you plan on doing long workouts, then plan your nutrient intake accordingly.

6. Stay positive: Don't let others demoralize you
It might take a little longer for vegans to build substantial body mass compared to non-vegans, but do not be discouraged. Just

keep exercising with a healthy frame of mind and concentrate on your goal. Take careful note of your food timings, supplements and workout strategy and you will definitely see the results of your efforts.

Chapter 6: Vegan Protein Bar Recipes

1. Vegan Chocolate Almond Protein Bars

INGREDIENTS:

- Raw almonds (1 cup)
- Salt (1/4 teaspoon)
- Rolled oats (1 ½ cups)
- Cinnamon (1 teaspoon)
- plant-based vanilla protein powder (5 ounces)
- maple syrup (1/3 cup)
- vegan chocolate chips from trader joes (1/4 cup)

DIRECTIONS:

1. Coat an 8x8-inch pan with parchment paper or cooking spray.
2. Cut ¼ cup of almonds into small pieces and set aside as it will be used as topping later on.
3. Add the remaining ¾ cup of almonds and the salt to a food blender and process for several minutes until the almonds have been finely powdered.
4. Now add in the maple syrup, the oats and the protein powder to the processed almonds and salt. Blend again until all ingredients are mixed well.
5. Pour the smooth mixture for the bars into the lined pan and level it out with a spoon. Then add the chopped almonds and push them into the mixture.
6. Melt the chocolate chips in a microwave until completely melted. Spread the chocolate on the bars and refrigerate for at least twenty minutes. After cooling, cut into bars.
7. The bars can be stored in an airtight container in the fridge.

2. Soft and Chewy Protein Granola Bars

Prep time: 10 mins   **Cook time:** 20 mins   **Total time:** 30 mins

Yields: 12 bars

Ingredients:
- 2 cups rolled oats
- ½ cup vanilla protein powder (whey can also be used)
- 2 Tbsp. ground flax
- 1 tsp. cinnamon
- ¼ tsp. salt
- ¼ cup almond butter (or any nut butter)
- ¼ cup maple syrup
- ½ cup vanilla almond milk (or any vegan milk)
- 1 tsp. vanilla extract
- ⅓ cup vegan chocolate chips from trader joes

Instructions:
1. Spray an 8x8-inch pan with cooking spray and set it aside. Preheat the oven to 350F.
2. Mix flax, cinnamon, oats, salt and protein powder in a bowl and set aside.
3. In another bowl mix almond milk, maple syrup, vanilla and almond butter till completely dissolved into each other. Now add this mixture to the previous mixture and again stir to get one smooth mixture. Add in the chocolate chips.
4. Transfer the mixture to the baking pan and press down, smoothing it with a spatula.
5. Place the baking pan in the oven and heat until the sides become golden brown, approximately 18-20 minutes.
6. Remove the dish from the oven and cool for about 20 minutes then cut into bars.

3. Soft + Chewy Baked Granola Bars

Vegan, gluten-free, nut-free, oil-free, refined sugar-free, soy-free

Yield: 10-12 bars
Prep time: 10 minutes
Cook time: 25 minutes

Ingredients:
- gluten-free oats (3/4 cup)
- water (1 cup)
- packed pitted Medjool dates (3/4 cup)
- chia seeds (1/2 cup)
- raw sunflower seeds (1/4 cup)
- raw pumpkin seeds (1/4 cup)
- finely chopped, dried cranberries (1/4 cup)
- cinnamon (1 teaspoon)
- pure vanilla extract (1 teaspoon)
- fine grain salt (1/4 teaspoon)

Directions:
1. Heat the oven to 325°F. Line an 8x8-inch pan with parchment paper.
2. Blend the rolled oats in a blender at the highest speed so that a very fine powdered flour is obtained. Put the flour into a large bowl.
3. Soak the pitted dates in water for half an hour and then transfer to the blender. Mix well so that the dates make a very smooth and soft paste.
4. Add the dates and the other ingredients to the oat flour and mix everything together. Spread the mixture in the baking pan evenly.
5. Cook the mixture for about 23-25 minutes or until it has hardened. Let it stay in the pan for 5 minutes to cool. After that, lift out the entire block, let it cool for another 5-10 minutes and then form bars.

4. Triple Layered Protein Bars with Peanut Butter and Chocolate

Bottom layer:
- Overnight soaked cashews (1 ¾ cup)
- Dry plums (¾ cup)
- Dutch processed cocoa powder (2 tbsp)
- Chia seeds (20g)
- Old fashioned oats (50g)
- Salt (1/4 teaspoon)
- Pure vanilla extract

Middle layer:
- Creamy peanut butter (250g)
- Peanut butter flavored protein powder (140g)

Top layer:
- Dutch processed cocoa powder (25g)
- Organic maple syrup (50g)
- Melted coconut oil (60g)
- Few roughly chopped, roasted, salted peanuts

Method:
For the Bottom layer:
Drain the water from the soaked cashews and put them in a blender. Also add the dried plums and blend to obtain a sticky paste. Then add in all the other ingredients and blend well. After everything is mixed well level it out at the bottom of a 28x12 cm pan which has been lined with parchment paper.

For the Middle layer:
Whip the creamy peanut butter till it is silky and fluffy. Then add the peanut butter protein powder in it. Transfer this mixture to the pan and flatten well.

For the Top layer:
In a bowl, add the syrup, melted coconut and cocoa powder and mix them all well together so that they have a creamy texture. Pour the mixture into the pan with the other two layers already spread and then top it with the small pieces of peanuts. Wrap the

dish in plastic wrap and refrigerate for about 4 hours, after which the bars can be cut out.

5. Maca Energy Bars

Prep Time: 10 minutes
Cook Time: 10 minutes
Total Time: 1 hour, 20 minutes

Ingredients:

- almonds (1 cup)
- sunflower seeds (1/2 cup)
- flax meal (1/2 cup)
- pepitas (1/2 cup)
- chia seeds (2 tablespoon)
- maca powder (2 tablespoon)
- maple syrup (1/4 cup)
- coconut oil (1/4 cup)
- almond butter (1/3 cup)
- sea salt (1/2 teaspoon)

Instructions:

1. Add almonds to a food processor and grind until coarsely powdered.
2. In a bowl mix the grinded almonds, salt, maca powder, pepitas, chia seeds, flax meal and sunflower seeds.
3. Heat the almond butter, maple syrup and coconut oil in a saucepan and mix thoroughly.
4. Transfer the ingredients from the saucepan to the bowl containing the other ingredients and combine.
5. Take an 8x8-inch pan lined with parchment paper and level the mixture into it, pressing down firmly.
6. Refrigerate for an hour. Then cut out the bars. The bars can be stored in the fridge or the freezer.

6. No Bake Protein Bars

Ingredients:
- oat flour (1 cup)
- vanilla protein powder (1 cup)
- Rice chex cereal (1 cup)
- chia seeds (2 tablespoon)
- soy milk (1/4 cup)
- peanut butter (½ cup)
- maple syrup (to taste or ideally 3-4 tablespoon)
- water (1-2 tablespoon)
- vegan chocolate chips (trader joes) (3 tablespoon)

Instructions:
1. Blend the flour, chia seeds, protein powder and cereal in a bowl.
2. In another bowl mix the milk, syrup and peanut butter. Microwave for about a minute, stirring once in between.
3. Mix the two mixtures together. If the paste is not well moistened or is lumpy then add in the water as well. Make sure the mixture is smooth and velvety.
4. Line an 8x8-inch pan and transfer the mixture into it, smoothing and pressing.
5. Keep in the freezer for 18-20 minutes and then slice into bars. Melted chocolate chips can also be added if desired. These bars can be stored in the fridge or freezer in an air tight container.

Notes:
1. Unflavored protein powder can be used, but for this you might have to add more syrup for sweetness and lower the amount of soy milk.
2. Instead of Chex you can use any other cereal of your choice.
3. Peanut butter can be substituted by any nut butter you like.

7. Raw Pumpkin Hemp Seed Protein Bars

Prep time 20 mins
Cook time 2 hours
Total time 2 hours 20 mins
Makes 16 bars

Ingredients:
- pitted and packed medjool dates (1/2 cup)
- water (¼ cup)
- Dastony Hemp Seed Butter (½ cup)
- raw oats (2 cups)
- raw pumpkin seeds (¼ cup)
- chia seeds (2 tablespoon)
- vanilla extract (½ teaspoon)
- cinnamon (½ teaspoon)
- nutmeg (¼ teaspoon)
- salt (¼ teaspoon)

Instructions:
1. Use parchment paper to line an 8x8-inch pan.
2. Soak the dates in water for about half an hour and then put the dates and water in a food processor and process to get a soft, even paste.
3. Now merge the prepared paste with the hemp seed butter and stir. Mix again thoroughly after adding all the other ingredients as well.
4. Place the mixture in the pan and level it. Then put it in the fridge for about 2 hours and cut into bars. Store these bars in the freezer.

8. Quinoa Protein Bars

Ingredients:

- Quinoa (1/3 cup)
- water (2/3 cup)
- pitted dates (16-17)
- sliced, blanched almonds (½ cup)
- crunchy peanut butter(1/3 cup)
- vegan dark chocolate (ghiardelli intense dark chocolate bar is preffered)(¼ cup)
- maple syrup (1 tablespoon)

Method:

1. Wash quinoa thoroughly and add it to a saucepan with water. Heat on high flame until it boils and then lower the flame. Let the contents of the saucepan cook while covered for 15 minutes. Set aside until it cools and then place it in the fridge for 2 hours.

2. Blend dates in a blender till it becomes soft and transfer to a bowl.

3. Process the almonds in the blender until finely chopped. Add the cooled quinoa and the peanut butter to the almonds and process again till mixed well. Place the paste in the bowl with the dates.

4. Mix all the ingredients in the bowl thoroughly. Make bars out of this mixture with your hands.

5. In a saucepan, stir the chocolate and syrup together until the chocolate melts. Top the bars with this paste and refrigerate until the chocolate hardens.

9. Fudge Brownie Chocolate Protein Bars

Ingredients:

- black beans (3 1/2 cups)
- regular cocoa powder (1 1/3 tablespoon)
- vegan chocolate protein powder (biochem preferred) (3 ½ tablespoon)
- salt (1/4 tsp)
- pure maple syrup or agave (3 ½ tablespoon)
- sugar (2 tablespoon)
- coconut or vegetable oil (½ tablespoon)
- pure vanilla extract (1 tablespoon)
- baking powder (1/2 tsp)
- vegan chocolate chips (trader joes)(2/3 cup)

Instructions:

1. Heat the oven to 350F. Except for the chocolate chips, mix all ingredients together in a blender until combined completely.

2. Prepare a baking pan by spraying with cooking spray. You may mix the chocolate chips with the mixture or sprinkle them on top. Press the mixture into the pan.

3. Put the pan in the preheated oven and cook for 15-17 minutes. Cool down and pat lightly. Leave it in the fridge overnight.

4. When taken out the bars will have hardened and are ready to be cut. The bars can be kept in the refrigerator.

10. Date Walnut Protein Bars with Sea Salt
Ingredients:
- creamy or crunchy almond butter (½ cup)
- pure maple syrup (¼ cup)
- vanilla extract (1 teaspoon)
- oats (½ cup)
- chopped medjool dates (¼ cup)
- chopped walnuts (3 tablespoons)
- protein powder, preferably unflavored (6 tablespoon or 1.5 scoops)
- sea salt (1/8 teaspoon)
- wax or parchment paper

Directions:
1. Mix together vanilla, maple syrup, almond butter, sea salt and dates in a bowl. Mix again after adding the oats, protein powder and walnuts.
2. Line an 8x8-inch pan with parchment paper and then add and smooth down the mixture.
3. Place in the fridge to cool for an hour or so. The bars can then be cut.
4. Packing each bar separately in wax paper keeps the bars fresher. The bars can be stored in the freezer.

11. Chocolate Jelly and Peanut Butter Protein Fudge

Ingredients:

- Maple Syrup (3/4 cup)
- peanut butter (3/4 cup)
- vanilla extract (1 teaspoon)
- vegan chocolate protein powder (biochem preferred)(1/2 cup)
- diced dried cherries (1/3 cup)
- chopped peanuts (1/3 cup)

Method:

1. Line any available size baking pan with foil or grease it with the cooking spray. Finely chop the dried fruit and peanuts.

2. Heat the honey over medium flame in a pan and remove it just before the honey starts to boil. Blend the heated Maple Syrup and peanut butter and mix thoroughly. Take care while adding the vanilla extract as it may start bubbling, and stir well. Immediately start stirring after adding the protein powder to obtain a perfect mix. Then whip in the fruit and nuts.

3. Spread the mix in the parchment lined pan according to the thickness you desire. Freeze the mixture for an hour and a half. Remove from the freezer and set it aside if it becomes difficult to cut after taking out the dish.

4. These bars can be stored for a long time if frozen in an airtight container.

Notes, suggestions, variations:

- Any other flavor of protein powder can be used and different brands of the ingredients can also be used, but you might have to increase or decrease the amounts.
- Dried fruit of your choice can also be used. You may add more than one type of dried fruit or just prefer one.

- Instead of peanuts you may use any of your favorite nuts or seeds or omit it entirely.
- You can add other ingredients that you might enjoy with your bars, e.g. chocolate chips, cereal pieces, toffee bits or rolled oats.
- Replace each egg in a recipe with one tablespoon of flax seed meal and tablespoons of water. For pancakes, the eggs can be replaced by a tablespoon of baking powder. Other substitutes include apple sauce or mashed prunes or silken tofu or mashed potatoes.

12. Super Seed Chocolate Protein Bars

Ingredients:

- solid coconut oil (1 tablespoon)
- maple syrup (2 tablespoon)
- almond milk or other non dairy milk (2 tablespoon)
- vegan dark chocolate chips (Trader Joe's brand chocolate chips) (1/3 cup)
- vanilla extract (1/2 teaspoon)
- salt (a small pinch)
- pumpkin or sunflower seeds (2 tablespoon)
- chia seeds (2 tablespoon)
- flax seeds (2 tablespoon)
- hemp seeds or other seeds (2 tablespoon)
- sesame seeds (1/4 cup)
- protein powder of choice (4 or more tablespoon)
- cinnamon or ginger or cloves to taste (can be omitted)

Method:

1. Add coconut oil, almond milk and maple syrup to a cooking pan. Heat and stir until the mixture comes to a boil. Then turn off the heat and remove from stove.

2. Add the mixture to the chocolate. Keep aside for at least two minutes so that the chocolate melts, and then whip until all the ingredients are mixed well.
3. Add the vanilla and salt to the mixture.
4. In a blender, process the chia, pumpkin, hemp and flax seeds so they become coarsely grounded.
5. Mix together the seed mixture, sesame seeds and melted chocolate. Blend thoroughly.
6. Whisk well after adding the protein powder.
7. Level the mixture on the parchment paper lining the dish. Place in the freezer until hardened completely.
8. Cut into bars and refrigerate to store. It can also be wrapped separately and stored.

13. Cranberry-Orange Power Grab Protein Bars

Ingredients:

- rolled oats (1 cup)
- nut or seed butter (1/2 cup)
- non dairy milk (1 1/3 cups)
- vanilla vegan protein powder (1 1/3 cups)
- dried cranberries (1/3 cup)
- finely grated orange zest (2 teaspoon)

Directions:
1. Spray an 8x8-inch pan with a non-stick cooking spray or cover with foil.
2. Grind the rolled oats in a blender until finely powdered.
3. Add the butter and dairy free milk to the blender and whip till a smooth mixture is formed
4. Add the protein powder to the food processor and whisk well, with intervals in between to scrape the sides. Then manually stir in the orange zest and the cranberries.
5. Pour the mixture into the prepared pan and level. Cover with wax paper and place in fridge overnight until it hardens.

6. After removing the pan from the fridge, remove the hardened mixture from the pan and place on a cutting board. Slice into bars and for storage, refrigerate.

14. Vegan High Protein Bars
Preparation time: 10 minutes
Serving: 8 bars

Ingredients:
- fortified soy protein powder (1 cup)
- cocoa powder (6 tablespoon)
- ground flax seed (4 tablespoon)
- agave nectar (3 tablespoon)
- creamy peanut butter (6 tablespoon)
- water (1.5 cups)
- muesli cereal (1 cup)

Directions:
1. In a bowl, add the flax seeds, protein powder and cocoa and whip thoroughly. Then put in the peanut butter, water and agave nectar. Whisk all the ingredients together. All ingredients should be properly mixed to make tastier bars.
2. Make sure the mixture has a thick consistency and sticks together to form balls.
3. Knead the mixture after adding in the muesli. Combine well.
4. Transfer the dough to a rectangular pan lined with parchment paper. Cut into bars before refrigeration. The bars should be refrigerated until chilled completely. The bars can be stored by wrapping each bar individually in an airtight container.

15. Healthy Red Velvet Fudge Protein Bars

Ingredients:

- roasted beet puree (3/4 cup)
- stevia –herbal sweetener (3/4 cup)
- walnut butter (1/2 cup)
- unsweetened soy milk (1/2 cup)
- vanilla paste (1 teaspoon)
- vegan chocolate rice protein powder (nutribiotic) (10 scoops)
- oat flour (2/3 cup)
- pink Himalayan salt (1/8 teaspoon)

Instructions

1. Cover an 8x8-inch cooking pan with parchment paper.
2. Add the beet puree, nut butter, herbal sweetener, soy milk and vanilla paste to a blender. Whip the ingredients on low.
3. Beat the oat flour, salt and protein powder in a bowl.
4. Transfer this mixture to the blender and process until smooth.
5. Make sure the dough has a thick consistency.
6. Transfer the dough to the cooking pan and press down to level.
7. Place more parchment paper over the dough. Place in the fridge overnight. Cut into bars.

16. Healthy Matcha Green Tea Fudge Protein Bars (low sugar, low fat, gluten free, vegan)

Preparation time: 10 minutes
Cooking time: 10 minutes
Servings: 10 bars

Ingredients:
- natural roasted almond butter (1/3 cup)
- unsweetened vanilla almond milk (1 cup + 2 tablespoon)
- stevia - herbal sweetener extract (1 teaspoon)
- lemon flavor or almond flavor (10 drops)
- vanilla brown rice protein powder (8 scoops)
- oat flour (1/2 cup)
- organic matcha powder (4 teaspoon)
- vegan mini chocolate chips, melted (trader joes preferred)(2-4 ounces)

Instructions:

1. Use parchment paper to line an 8x8-inch brownie pan and then set aside.
2. Put the lemon flavor, almond butter, almond milk and stevia in a blender and process on low.
3. Thoroughly whip the matcha powder, protein powder and oat flour. Carefully pour the mixture into the blender.
4. Blend all the ingredients together until it forms a dough. Scrape the sides of the jug with a spatula.
5. Transfer the dough to the brownie pan and flatten it with either a rubber spatula or a pastry roller.
6. Wrap the dish in plastic wrap and place in fridge overnight.
7. Remove the pan after the prescribed time and cut into bars. Spread the melted chocolate chips on it.
8. For storage, either wrap it in plastic wrap or keep in an airtight container and refrigerate.

Notes:

The lemon flavor is added to enhance the flavor of the matcha powder. Instead of lemon flavor, almond flavor can be used. But if you do not add any, just increase the chocolate added.

Avoid using whey protein because it will give the dough a gooey texture and will not chill properly.

17. (Chocolate) Muesli Protein Bars
Servings: 8 bars
Ingredients:

- 1/2 cup unsweetened almond milk (or any unsweetened non-dairy milk)
- 3 tbsp maple syrup
- 1/2 ripe, mashed banana
- 1 tsp chia seeds
- 1/2 tsp cinnamon
- 1 1/2 cups Muesli Fusion
- 2 scoops vegan chocolate protein powder (biochem preferred)
- 1/4 cup sliced almonds, or roughly chopped full almonds (to be measured after chopping)
- 1/4 cup uncooked or partially cooked quinoa
- 1 tbsp flour (optional)

Directions:

1. Preheat oven to 350 degrees F.
2. Mix well first 4 ingredients in a medium-large bowl and blend. Set aside. Mix the dry ingredients in another bowl. When uniformly mixed all through, gradually add dry constituents to the bowl of wet ingredients, making certain all of it gets equally mixed. The mixture must be quite wet, but if you think it feels too wet, add a tablespoon of flour.
3. Preferably you should use an 8×8-inch or 9×9-inch pan for these bars. Cover your pan with oil and press the batter firmly into the pan. Bake for 20-25 minutes, checking regularly. You will want them to be solid in the

center, and to appear dry.

4. Remove from the stove and allow to cool a bit before removing from the pan. Cool completely to room temperature before cutting into bars.

5. Store in an airtight container, or wrap the bars separately in plastic wrap and keep in the fridge. Should keep for about a week.

18. Super Protein Star Crunch Bars

Prep time 10 mins

Cook time 10 mins

Total time 20 mins

High-protein hemp seeds, flax cereal, dark chocolate and caramel are combined to yield a crispy, protein-rich bar.

Recipe type: Dessert
Serves: 10

Ingredients:
- 5 ounces thick caramel sauce
- 1½ cups crunchy flax cereal
- 1 tablespoon butter
- 4 tablespoons hemp seeds (shelled)
- 12 ounces dark chocolate (Ghiardelli intense vegan dark chocolate)(melted)

Instructions:
1. Warm caramel sauce in a big pot over low heat until liquefied.
2. Blend in the hemp seeds and butter and stir until mixed.
3. Once removed from heat, add in the flax cereal and whip until uniformly covered with caramel mix.
4. Put spoonfuls of the mixture into a muffin tin (well-greased) and lightly compress to form patties (makes 10

patties). Place the muffin tin in the refrigerator for 30-45 minutes for the patties to set.

5. Place parchment paper on a baking sheet. Spread out the chilled patties and coat with the melted dark chocolate. Place it back onto the lined baking pan. Do the same with all caramel patties.

6. Chill for 25-30 minutes for chocolate to set.

7. Dish out and enjoy. Leftovers can be kept in the refrigerator.

19. Blueberry Breakfast Bars (Refined Sugar Free, Raw Vegan, Gluten Free)

Ingredients:
- 1 + 1/2 cups pure oats (gluten free)
- 3/4 cup almonds whole
- 1/2 cup heaping dried blueberries
- 1/2 cup pistachios
- 1/3 cup flaxseed (ground)
- 1/3 cup walnuts
- 1/3 cup pepitas
- 1/4 cup sunflower seeds
- 1/3 cup pure maple syrup
- 1/4 cup apple sauce (unsweetened)
- 1 cup almond butter

Notes: You can add any nut/seed of your choice or dried fruit that you wish. Dates, figs, cherries, cranberries & sliced apricots are all delicious substitutes.

Directions:

1. Cover an 8x 8-inch baking pan with wax or parchment paper so that the paper falls over the edges.

2.	Mix the first 8 ingredients in a large bowl and blend properly.

3.	Now incorporate syrup, apple sauce and mix. Add almond butter to the mixture.

4.	Place batter in the prepared pan, pressing down firmly with palm of hands and spreading as evenly as possible.

5.	Place the pan in the freezer for around an hour.

6.	Remove pan from freezer. Raise each portion from the pan by lifting up the paper. Place slab down and lightly peel paper away. Slice slab into bars. Keep chilled in a sealed container/plastic bag in the freezer.

Disclaimer:

This recipes and information in this book are not intended as a substitute for the medical advice of physicians. The reader should regularly consult a physician in matters relating to his/her health and particularly with respect to any symptoms that may require diagnosis or medical attention.

Copyright @ ProjectVegan Inc. / Tadro Labitad.

Conclusion:

More and more people are adopting the vegan lifestyle, and it certainly does not mean you have to to sacrifice your fitness or muscle building goals. Vegetable protein diets can be constructed effectively for athletes and bodybuilders, as many have established. Consideration of details is vital for total energy, protein, essential fats, vitamin B12 and minerals like iron, calcium and zinc. I hope the readers of this book will be convinced of the benefits of a vegan diet and also learn of the importance of protein in your daily diet, rich sources of vegetarian protein and even non-vegans can enjoy these scrumptious protein bars.

Printed in Great Britain
by Amazon